THE UNRAVELING OF THE BUSH PRESIDENCY

THE
UNRAVELING
OF THE
BUSH
PRESIDENCY

HOWARD ZINN

SEVEN STORIES PRESS
NEW YORK • LONDON • MELBOURNE • TORONTO

Seven Stories Press
140 Watts Street
New York, NY 10013
http://www.sevenstories.com

In Canada: Publishers Group Canada, 559 College Street, Suite 402, Toronto, ON M6G 1A9

In the U.K.: Turnaround Publisher Services Ltd., Unit 3, Olympia Trading Estate, Coburg Road, Wood Green, London N22 6TZ

In Australia: Palgrave Macmillan, 627 Chapel Street, South Yarra, VIC 3141

College professors may order examination copies of Seven Stories Press titles for a free six-month trial period. To order, visit http://www.sevenstories.com/textbook/ or send a fax on school letterhead to 212.226.1411.

Library of Congress Cataloging-in-Publication Data
Zinn, Howard, 1922-
   The unraveling of the Bush presidency / Howard Zinn.
      p. cm.
   ISBN 978-1-58322-769-5 (pbk.)
1. United States--Politics and government--2001- 2. United States--Foreign relations--2001- 3. United States--Social policy--1993- 4. Political corruption--United States. 5. Bush, George W. (George Walker), 1946---Political and social views. 6. Iraq War, 2003- I. Title.

E902.Z48 2007
973.931--dc22

2007010485

Book design by Jon Gilbert
Printed in Canada.

9 8 7 6 5 4 3 2 1

The last edition of *A People's History of the United States* ends with the election of 2000. In that election, the Democratic candidate, Al Gore, received hundreds of thousands of votes more than George Bush, but in the State of Florida, whose governor was George Bush's brother, the official in charge of counting votes was a leading Republican, and she declared Bush the winner by a tiny margin. She refused to have a recount though thousands of votes were not counted, especially in districts of black voters. The Florida Supreme Court overruled her, ordering a full recount, but the Supreme Court of the United States, by a five to four vote (all five being Republican appointees) refused a recount, leaving Bush the winner.

My *People's History* also ends with the tragedy of September 11, 2001, when hijackers crashed their planes into the World Trade Center in New York, killing close to three thousand people. Bush immediately declared a "war on terrorism" and proclaimed, "We shall make no distinction between terrorists and countries that harbor terrorism." The Senate and the House of Representatives approved a resolution giving Bush the power to take military action, with only one member of Congress, an African-American representative from California, Barbara Lee, refusing to give her consent.

On the supposition that the hijackings had been ordered by the militant Islamic group Al Qaeda, whose leader was Osama Bin Laden, United States forces bombed and invaded Afghanistan. Bin Laden was never captured, and the Al Qaeda organization remained alive, but in the military operation thousands of Afghan civilians were killed, and hundreds of thousands forced from their homes.

The terrible toll of human life in the invasion was justified on the ground that it removed the Taliban, a fundamentalist Islamic group that ruled Afghanistan with an iron hand, and was responsible for countless atrocious acts against the population. However, the defeat of the Taliban brought into power the Northern Alliance, which had been responsible in the mid-'90s for many acts of violence against the people of Kabul and other Afghan cities.

George Bush, in his 2002 State of the Union Address, claimed that with the ouster of the Taliban, "Today women are free." But this was a false claim, according to an organization of Afghan women. The *New York Times* reporter, Nicholas Kristoff, two years after the invasion, reported that Afghan women were not free. Although he had supported the U.S. attack on Afghanistan, he now felt "betrayed, as do the Afghans themselves." He found that "banditry and chaos are rampant, longtime warlords control much of the country, the Taliban is having a resurgence in the southeast" and he quoted a U.N. report worrying that Afghanistan would soon be in the hands of "drug cartels and narco-terrorists."

Sixteen months into the war, a Scotsman who took medical aid to thirteen Afghan villages was distressed at what he saw: "The country is on its knees. . . . It is one of the most heavily land-mined countries in the world . . . 25% of all children are dead by the age of five." He concluded, sadly: "Surely, at the start of our 21st century, we should have evolved beyond the point where we reduce a country and a people to dust, for the flimsiest of excuses."

As late as August of 2006, air strikes were still killing Afghan civilians, and the *New York Times* reported "corruption, violence and poverty" were widespread in the country.

It was clear that the military attack on Afghanistan had neither brought democracy or security, or weakened terrorism. In fact, in his State of the Union address in January 2002, President Bush, while claiming that "we are winning the war on terror," admitted that "tens of thousands of trained terrorists are still at large." Indeed, if anything, the violence unleashed by the United States, angering people in the Middle East, had increased the number of terrorists.

With Afghanistan still in turmoil, the Bush administration began to set the stage for a war against Iraq. Richard Clarke, adviser to the president on matters of terrorism, reported later that immediately after the attacks of 9-11, the White House was looking for reasons to attack Iraq, though there was no evidence linking Iraq to those attacks.

Starting in 2002, George Bush and the officials closest to him, Vice President Dick Cheney, Secretary of Defense Donald Rumsfeld, and National Security Advisor Condoleeza Rice, began a campaign to persuade the public that Iraq and its dictator, Saddam Hussein, constituted a serious threat to the United States and to the world. They accused Iraq of concealing "weapons of mass destruction," including plans to build a nuclear weapon.

A United Nations inspection team, making hundreds of inspections all over Iraq, was unable to find these weapons. There was no evidence of Iraq working on a nuclear weapon, but Vice President Cheney insisted it was a fact, and Condoleeza Rice spoke menacingly of "a mushroom cloud," invoking the picture of the atomic bombing of Hiroshima. A climate of hysteria was created. The government pointed to atrocities committed by Saddam Hussein, including the massacre of 5,000 Iraqi Kurds by the use of chemical poisons. In fact, Hussein was a monstrous tyrant, but when the killing of the Kurds took place in 1988 the United States raised no strenuous objections. It saw Iraq as an ally, and supported its war against Iran.

What was the real reason for the build-up of a war atmosphere against Iraq? It was not credible that Iraq, a country ruined by two wars (In the 1980s against Iran, in 1991 the invasion by the United States) and devastated by ten years of economic sanctions, was a threat to the greatest military power on earth.

Much more likely as a reason for war was that Iraq possessed the second largest oil reserves in the world (Saudi Arabia was first), and the United States, ever since the end of World War II, was determined to control the oil of the Middle East. That motive was behind the U.S. actions when, in 1953, it overthrew a government in Iran which nationalized its oil industry. The result of the coup was to restore to power the dictatorship of the Shah. Oil continued to govern U.S. policy in the region whether Democrats or Republicans were in the White House. Indeed, it was in the administration of the liberal Democrat Jimmy Carter that the "Carter Doctrine" was enunciated, declaring that the United States would defend its interest in Middle East oil "by any means necessary, including military force."

None of this, however, was told to the public. It was part of a historic pattern in U.S. foreign policy to tell the American people that war was necessary to defend the United States against a threat, or to bring liberty and democracy to other countries, while the real motives for war—the profits of corporations, the control of vital raw materials, the expansion of the U.S. empire—were concealed.

The Bush administration hoped to get the United Nations to support a war against Iraq, but the other members of the Security Council were not convinced, even though Secretary of State Colin Powell gave a speech to the U.N.—later exposed as false information—listing the weapons of mass destruction he claimed were possessed by Saddam Hussein.

In a document called "National Security Strategy" issued in September 2002, the Bush administration had declared its determination to take military action unilaterally, that is, without international support, whenever it felt this necessary to maintain its supremacy in the world. This was a violation of the Charter of the United Nations, which allowed military action only in self-defense, and only when approved by the Security Council.

Nevertheless, the United States prepared through the winter of 2002 and the spring of 2003 to make war on Iraq. All over the world there was opposition to this. On February 15, 2003, there were simultaneous demonstrations across the globe, involving ten to fifteen million people protesting against the impending war. A *New York Times* article, commenting on these demonstrations, said: "There are now two superpowers in the world—the United States, and world public opinion."

Despite the protests, on March 20, 2003, the United States government launched a massive attack, by land and air, dropping thousands of bombs, and sending over 100,000 soldiers into Iraq, calling it "Operation Iraqi Freedom." The intensity of the violence was represented by the phrase "shock and awe." Hundreds of U.S. soldiers were killed, thousands of Iraqis died, many of them civilians.

After three weeks, the city of Baghdad was occupied. By May 1, six weeks after the invasion, major military operations were declared over, and President George Bush stood triumphantly on an aircraft carrier, with a huge banner behind him: "Mission Accomplished."

In fact, if the mission was to take control of Iraq, it was not accomplished. Violence continued, indeed grew, as insurgents carried out attacks against the U.S. occupying army. Saddam Hussein was captured in December of 2003, but this did nothing to stop the attacks. The Bush administration pointed to elections taking place in Iraq as a sign of democracy, but the elections put one faction in power (the Shiites) and left the former ruling group (the Sunnis) out of power, leading to more violence.

The occupation became more and more resented by the Iraqis. U.S. troops were rounding up Iraqi men suspected of being insurgents, holding thousands without any charges, without any judicial process. A year after the invasion, photos appeared showing that U.S. troops were torturing Iraqi prisoners at the Abu Ghraib prison, and there was evidence that this had the approval of Secretary of Defense Donald Rumsfeld. When the Senate was considering a bill to ban torture, Vice President Cheney visited senators to argue against the bill. All this further inflamed hostility against the U.S. Polls among the Iraqis showed that a vast majority of the Iraqis wanted U.S. troops out of Iraq.

President Bush and his administration refused to consider withdrawing from Iraq. We must "stay the course," Bush said. We must not "cut and run," Vice President Cheney and Secretary of Defense Donald Rumsfeld declared. Meanwhile, U.S. casualties were mounting, and by the middle of 2006 there were over 2,500 dead, and tens of thousands more wounded. These wounds were often severe, requiring amputations of arms and legs, and causing blindness. The administration went to great lengths to keep the American public from seeing the coffins, and to keep out of sight the armless and legless veterans.

There were far more casualties among the Iraqis. By mid 2006, after three years of war, hundreds of thousands of Iraqis had died, and Iraqi society was in a shambles, with people deprived of clean water, of electricity, living in a situation of continuing violence and chaos.

When the war began, a large majority of the American people, the memory of the September 11 disaster still fresh, accepted the Bush administration's argument that Saddam Hussein had "weapons of mass destruction" and that action against Iraq was part of the "war on terror." There was no questioning of this by the major organs of press and television, and the Democratic Party largely supported the war and the Bush policies, so that the public was largely uninformed.

However, as the war went on, the situation became more and more clear. The war had brought neither democracy, nor freedom, nor security to the people of Iraq. The government of the United States had deceived the American people about "weapons of mass destruction" which did not exist, had magnified the threat from Saddam Hussein far beyond the reality, had claimed a connection with the events of 9-11, which had no basis in fact. It had supported torture and the detention without trial of thousands of people in Iraq and in the United States.

And the death toll in Iraq, for both Americans and Iraqis, kept growing.

Furthermore, the Bush administration was using the war as a justification for violating the constitutional rights of the people of the United States. Six weeks after 9-11, it had passed the PATRIOT Act, a 342 page document that Congress had little time to read and yet, in the heated atmosphere of 9-11, the House of Representatives approved it by an overwhelming majority and the Senate passed it with only one dissenting vote.

Its very title suggested that anyone who opposed it was unpatriotic. The act extended the power of the government to intercept communications, and gave government agencies the power to search people's homes without their knowledge. This was similar to the "Writs of Assistance," which was one of the grievances that the American colonists had against the British, leading up to the Revolutionary War.

Shortly after 9-11, the United States began picking up people in Afghanistan and other places whom it accused of terrorism and instead of treating them as prisoners of war, which would have required giving them the rights required by international law, created a category of "unlawful enemy combatants" and locked them up in Guantánamo Bay, the U.S. military installation at the edge of Cuba. They were given no trial, and were not told what the charges were against them. Soon, reports of torture began to emerge.

After many hunger strikes and suicide attempts, in June of 2006 three of the prisoners committed suicide.

A United Nations Committee Against Torture reported on U.S. policies at Guantánamo and elsewhere, and said that the U.S. should close the Guantánamo facility. It further pointed to evidence that the United States was sending detainees to other countries, where their whereabouts could not be traced, and where many of them were being tortured.

In the fall of 2006, Congress passed, and President Bush signed, a bill permitting the CIA to continue harsh interrogation of suspected terrorists in secret prisons abroad. The bill also eliminated the right of habeas corpus for anyone designated by the president or the secretary of defense as an "unlawful enemy combatant"—even U.S. citizens. That is, people detained would not have the right to be brought before a court to challenge their arrest.

The war in Iraq was now costing hundreds of billions of dollars. The military budget passed unanimously by Congress in 2006 called for an expenditure of 500 billion dollars—half a trillion—the largest military budget in history. Meanwhile, cuts were being made in funds for education and medical care. And huge profits were being made by corporations getting military contracts from the government. The price of gasoline had risen to record levels, while the Exxon

Corporation was reporting annual profits of forty billion dollars.

The C.E.O.s (Chief Executive Officers) of Corporations were making enormous salaries, four hundred times the wage of the average worker, while the minimum wage for working people remained as it had been for ten years, at $5.15 an hour. There was an outcry even on the business pages of the *New York Times*, where financial writer Bob Stein asked: "Is this America, where far too many of the rich endlessly loot their stockholders and kick the employees in the teeth, the America that our soldiers in Ramadi and Kirkuk and Anbar Province and Afghanistan are fighting for . . . the America that our men and women are losing limbs for, coming home in boxes for?"

The resistance of the American people to this situation grew slowly but steadily as the war went on. Anti-war rallies, vigils, protests took place all over the country, never reaching the scale of the huge anti-war demonstrations that marked the Vietnam era, but symbolic of the growing alienation of the public from the policies of the Bush administration.

Cindy Sheehan, a California mother whose son Casey died in Iraq, spoke out powerfully against the war, and when she camped out near Bush's ranch home in Crawford, Texas she drew support from all over the country. In a speech she made to a Veterans for Peace gathering in Dallas, she

Anti-war activist Cindy Sheehan speaks to the news media at the
White House, 2005. CORBIS

addressed George Bush as follows: "You tell me the truth. You tell me that my son died for oil. You tell me that my son died to make your friends rich. You tell me my son died so you can spread the cancer of Pax Americana, imperialism in the Middle East."

As the war in Iraq continued, young people who joined the military began to reconsider. A year into the war, a young woman in Illinois, Diedra Cobb, filed a claim as a conscientious objector. She wrote: "I joined the Army thinking that I was, quite possibly, upholding some of the mightiest of ideals for the greatest, most powerful country on this earth. . . . There had to be some good that would come out of the carnage, in the end. But this is where I made my mistake, because in war there is no end. We are still in Germany, we are still in Korea, we are still in Bosnia, hell, we're still in America. The list goes on, and the only things that are determined are who will stay and who will go, who will live and who will die, who will rule, and who will serve. I did not know that peace cannot come from war because war never ends."

By the end of 2004, a CBS news story reported that 5,500 soldiers had deserted since the start of the war a year and a half before. Many had gone to Canada. One of them, Jimmy Massey, a former marine staff sergeant seeking asylum, told a hearing in Toronto that he and his fellow marines shot and killed more than thirty unarmed men, women, and children, and even shot a young Iraqi who got out of his car with his arms in the air.

Around the same time, a *New York Times* story said: "The army has encountered resistance from more than 2,000 former soldiers it has ordered back to military work." The military was getting desperate about filling the ranks as soldiers in Iraq came to the end of their promised term. The newspaper *The Independent* in England reported on U.S. deserters: "Sergeant Kevin Benderman cannot shake the images from his head. There are bombed villages and desperate people. There are dogs eating corpses thrown into a mass grave. And most unremitting of all, there is the image of a young Iraqi girl, no more than eight or nine, one arm severely burnt and blistered, and the sound of her screams."

In the fall of 2006, a group called Citizen Soldier opened "The Different Drummer Internet Café" in Watertown, New York, offering GIs from a large military base nearby a place where they could use the Internet, drink coffee, and share views on the war. During the Vietnam War, there were a dozen "GI Coffeehouses" set up near military bases, where soldiers could come, exchange information, get anti-war literature, listen to music.

As it became more difficult for the military to persuade young people to join, the efforts to recruit teenagers became more intense, with recruiters visiting high schools, approaching students at football games and in school cafeterias. At the same time, anti-war groups began a campaign to counter the pro-war propaganda of the recruiters. Counter-recruiters visited schools in Chicago, New York, Los Angeles, Portland (Oregon), San Francisco and other cities.

By 2006 the anti-war activity in the nation had not reached the high point of activism during the war in Vietnam, but it clearly was increasing. There were vigils and meetings in hundreds of towns and cities around the country, and some people engaged in acts of civil disobedience to dramatize opposition to the war. For instance, in New York City in April of 2006, eighteen members of the

"Granny Peace Brigade" blocked the entrance to a military recruiting center in Times Square. They were arrested, charged with disorderly conduct, but at their trial the judge, after listening to the women, ages fifty-nine to ninety-one, testify as to why they had acted as they did, decided they had been wrongly arrested.

By this time, three years of war in Iraq had turned a population that initially supported the war to a majority that opposed the war and declared their lack of confidence in President Bush. One of the signs of the new mood was that some journalists who worked for prominent newspapers, which had gone along with the war, began to speak out boldly. Andy Rooney, on the very popular television show *Sixty Minutes*, declared, to an audience of many millions on Memorial Day, May 30, 2006, noting that he himself was a veteran of World War II: "We use the phrase 'gave their lives,' but they didn't give their lives. Their lives were taken from them. . . . I wish we could dedicate Memorial Day, not to the memory of those who have died at war, but to the idea of saving the lives of the young people who are going to die in the future if we don't find some new way—some new religion maybe—that takes war out of our lives."

The veteran journalist Helen Thomas, whose face and voice were known to all Americans who watched the television program *Meet The Press*, wrote a newspaper column, saying: "We don't need more phony timetables to prolong the agony. We need a quick exit from a bad show." She pointed to the feeble response to the war of the Democratic Party. "Where is the opposition in the opposition party?"

While the government was trying to intimidate Americans into silence, people still spoke up. Librarians in California shredded their records rather than disclose the names of book borrowers to the FBI. At least two hundred of 1,500 libraries surveyed said they had not cooperated with law enforcement authorities in giving out records.

People in the arts spoke up against the war. The well-known singers, the Dixie Chicks, stood by their lead singer, Natalie Maines, when she defended a statement made in Europe that she was ashamed to be from Bush's home state of Texas. Although hundreds of radio stations then refused to play their music, they continued to bring huge crowds to their concerts and to sell large numbers of their recordings.

In the supposedly conservative Salt Lake City, the mayor, "Rocky" Anderson, was cheered by thousands when he called President Bush a "dishonest, war-mongering, human-rights violating president," and said that this would "rank as the worst presidency our nation has ever had to endure."

In the fiercely nationalistic atmosphere which the Bush administration tried hard to maintain, one of the results was a wave of resentment against millions of immigrants,

Protesters in holding a massive American flag during the immigration rally in downtown Dallas, 2006. CORBIS

especially Mexicans, who had come to the United States, who did not have legal status, and who were seen as taking jobs from people in the United States. Although various studies showed that these immigrants did not hurt, but helped the economy, anti-immigration feeling rose, especially in the Southwest section of the country.

Congress approved plans to build a 750-mile fence along the southern borders of California and Arizona, to keep out Mexicans who were trying to escape poverty in their home country. The irony seemed lost on the U.S. government—that it was working so strenuously to keep poor Mexican people from coming into territory that had been seized from Mexico in the war of 1846–48.

As legislation was being discussed in Congress to punish people who were in this country illegally, there were huge demonstrations around the country in the spring of 2005, especially in California and the Southwest, involving hundreds of thousands of people demanding equal rights for immigrants. Not only immigrants themselves, but Americans who supported them, joined these actions. A common slogan was: "No Human Being Is Illegal."

In the midst of growing opposition to the policies of the Bush administration, at home and abroad, disaster struck in New Orleans, Louisiana, in August of 2005, in the form of a deadly hurricane which smashed the levees protecting the city from the Mississippi

River, destroyed much of the city, brought death and injury to thousands, and left hundreds of thousands of people homeless. A *Washington Post* reporter wrote:

"People around the world cannot believe what they're seeing. From Argentina to Zimbabwe, front-page photos of the dead and desperate in New Orleans, almost all of them poor and black, have sickened them, and shaken assumptions about American might. How can this be happening, they ask, in a nation whose wealth and power seem almost supernatural in so many struggling corners of the world. . . . International reaction has shifted in many cases from shock, sympathy and generosity to a growing criticism of the Bush administration's response to the catastrophe of Hurricane Katrina."

The same reporter wrote that ". . . many people see at best incompetence and at worst racism in the chaos gripping much of the Gulf Coast. Many analysts said President Bush's focus on Iraq had left the United States without resources to handle natural disasters, and many said Hurricane Katrina's fury mocked Bush's opposition to international efforts to confront global warning, which some experts say contributes to the severity of such storms."

The Katrina experience pointed to a larger conclusion about United States policy—that while millions of people in Africa and Asia, and even poor people in the United States, were dying of malnutrition and sickness, while natural disasters were taking huge tolls of life all over the world (as with the Tsunami earthquake in Southeast Asia in 2004), the United States government was pouring its enormous wealth into war and the building of empire.

There were many issues on the minds of people in the United States as they went to the polls in November of 2006 to elect the members of the House of Representatives and one third of the members of the Senate. But undoubtedly, uppermost in their thinking was the disaster going on in Iraq, and the wealth of the nation being drained by the requirements of the war. In the face of President Bush's suggestions that the Social Security System be put in private hands, a million Americans signed petitions asking that the system be saved.

The result of the 2006 election, in which Democrats won control of the House and Senate by a narrow margin, was a repudiation of the Bush administration more than a show of enthusiasm for the Democrats. Still, as Democratic candidates strongly opposed to the war won enough seats for the victory, it was a dramatic indication of the change in public opinion about the war and the recognition of so many people that the Bush administration represented mainly the interests of the wealthy classes. It was a rare democratic moment in the recent history of the nation.

HOWARD ZINN is professor emeritus at Boston University. He is the author of the classic *A People's History of the United States*, "a brilliant and moving history of the American people from the point of view of those . . . whose plight has been largely omitted from most histories" (*Library Journal*), and coauthor (with Anthony Arnove) of its companion volume, *Voices of a People's History of the United States*.

Zinn has received the Lannan Foundation Literary Award for Nonfiction and the Eugene V. Debs award for his writing and political activism, and in 2003 was awarded the Prix des amis du Monde Diplomatique.

Zinn is the author of numerous books, including *The Zinn Reader*, the autobiographical *You Can't Be Neutral on a Moving Train*, and the play *Marx in Soho*.

Zinn grew up in Brooklyn and worked in the shipyards before serving as an air force bombardier in World War II. Zinn was chair of the History Department at Spelman College, where he actively participated in the civil rights movement, before taking a position at Boston University. While there he became a leader in the movement to end the war in Vietnam.

He now lives with his wife, Roslyn, in Massachusetts and lectures widely on history, contemporary politics, and against war.

His most recent book is *A Young People's History of the United States*.

ALSO BY HOWARD ZINN

A Young People's History of the United States, with Rebecca Stefoff. New York: Seven Stories Press, 2007.

A Power Governments Cannot Suppress. San Francisco, City Lights, 2006.

Voices of a People's History of the United States, with Anthony Arnove. New York: Seven Stories Press, 2004.

Artists in Times of War. New York: Seven Stories Press, 2003.

Passionate Declarations: Essays on War and Justice. New York: Harper Perennial, 2003.

You Can't Be Neutral on a Moving Train: A Personal History of Our Times, 2d ed. Boston: Beacon Press, 2002.

Terrorism and War, with Anthony Arnove. New York: Seven Stories Press, 2002.

Emma. Cambridge: South End Press, 2002.

A People's History of the United States: 1492–Present, updated ed. New York: HarperCollins/Perennial Classics, 2001.

Three Strikes: Miners, Musicians, Salesgirls, and the Fighting Spirit of Labor's Last Century, with Dana Frank and Robin D. G. Kelley. Boston: Beacon Press, 2001.

Howard Zinn on War. New York: Seven Stories Press, 2001.

Howard Zinn on History. New York: Seven Stories Press, 2001.

La otra historia de los Estados Unidos. New York: Seven Stories Press, 2001.

Marx in Soho: A Play on History. Cambridge: South End Press, 1999.

The Future of History: Interviews with David Barsamian. Monroe, Maine: Common Courage Press, 1999.

The Zinn Reader: Writings on Disobedience and Democracy. New York: Seven Stories Press, 1997.

Failure to Quit: Reflections of an Optimistic Historian. Monroe, Maine: Common Courage Press, 1993. Reprint ed., Cambridge: South End Press, 2002.

The Politics of History, 2d ed. Urbana: University of Illinois Press, 1990.

Justice: Eyewitness Accounts. Boston: Beacon Press, 1977. Reprint ed., Cambridge: South End Press, 2002.

Postwar America: 1945–1971. Indianapolis: Bobbs-Merrill, 1973. Reprint ed., Cambridge: South End Press, 2002.

Disobedience and Democracy: Nine Fallacies of Law and Order. New York: Vintage Books, 1968. Reprint ed., Cambridge: South End Press, 2002.

Vietnam: The Logic of Withdrawal. Boston: Beacon Press, 1967. Reprint ed., Cambridge: South End Press, 2002.

SNCC: The New Abolitionists. Boston: Beacon Press, 1964. Reprint ed., Cambridge: South End Press, 2002.

The Southern Mystique. New York: Knopf, 1964. Reprint ed. Cambridge: South End Press, 2002.

LaGuardia in Congress. Ithaca, NY: Cornell University Press, 1959.

ABOUT SEVEN STORIES PRESS

Seven Stories Press is an independent book publisher based in New York City, with distribution throughout the United States, Canada, England, and Australia. We publish works of the imagination by such writers as Nelson Algren, Octavia E. Butler, Assia Djebar, Ariel Dorfman, Barry Gifford, Lee Stringer, and Kurt Vonnegut, to name a few, together with political titles by voices of conscience, including the Boston Women's Health Book Collective, Noam Chomsky, Ralph Nader, Gary Null, Project Censored, Barbara Seaman, Gary Webb, and Howard Zinn, among many others. Our books appear in hardcover, paperback, pamphlet, and e-book formats, in English and in Spanish. We believe publishers have a special responsibility to defend free speech and human rights, and to celebrate the gifts of the human imagination, wherever we can.

For more information about us, visit our Web site at www.sevenstories.com or write for a free catalogue to Seven Stories Press, 140 Watts Street, New York, NY 10013.